12/21

ME and my WORLD

My Family

Written by C.J. Polin

Illustrated by Ryan Wheatcroft

W
FRANKLIN WATTS

Franklin Watts

First published in Great Britain in 2021
by The Watts Publishing Group
© The Watts Publishing Group 2021

Editors: Sarah Peutrill and Sarah Ridley
Design: Anthony Hannant (Little Red Ant)

ISBN: 978 1 4451 7340 5 (hbk)
ISBN: 978 1 4451 7345 0 (pbk)

The text in this book was previously published in All About Me: My Family by Caryn Jenner but has been updated, revised and newly designed and illustrated for this new publication.

The website addresses (URLs) included in this book were valid at the time of going to press. However, it is possible that contents or addresses may have changed since the publication of this book. No responsibility for any such changes can be accepted by either the author or the Publisher.

Printed in Dubai

Franklin Watts
An imprint of Hachette Children's Group
Part of The Watts Publishing Group
Carmelite House
50 Victoria Embankment
London EC4Y 0DZ
An Hachette UK Company

www.hachette.co.uk
www.franklinwatts.co.uk

FSC
MIX
Paper from responsible sources
FSC® C104740
www.fsc.org

CONTENTS

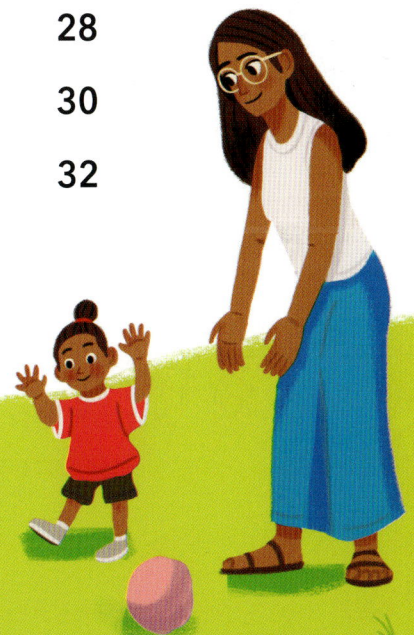

PART OF THE FAMILY

We are all part of a family. Families can be big or small and every family is different and special.

This family has a mum and two children. Who is in your family?

The People in a Family

Families are made up of lots of different people – mums and dads, step-dads and step-mums, sisters, brothers, cousins, grannies, grandads and more. Some people have big families and others have small families. The people that you live with are your immediate family.

Family Tree

You probably have lots of family members – or relatives – who do not live with you. There are your grandparents, aunts, uncles and cousins and they are your extended family. They are all part of your family tree – and the tree gets bigger and bigger as it branches out to include more relatives.

Grandma, Grandpa Jo and Grandpa
(Dad's mum, step-dad and dad)

Granny and Grandad
(Mum's mum and dad)

Mum

My brother

Me

Dad

This is Laura's family tree. It shows her immediate family plus her grandparents. On pages 16-17 there is a family tree showing all of her extended family.

PARENTS

Most children have parents or carers who look after them. Children may live with their mum and dad, with two mums or dads, with one parent, or with one parent and their partner. Some children live with their grandparents. Sometimes children move from one family to the other on different days of the week.

New to the Family

Most parents have a baby because they love each other and now they want to love a child as well. Some parents are happy with one child while others have several. Whatever the size of family, when a new baby arrives in the home, family life changes.

Leo lives with his mum and his step-dad. His mum is pregnant with another baby. Leo wonders what it will be like to be a big brother.

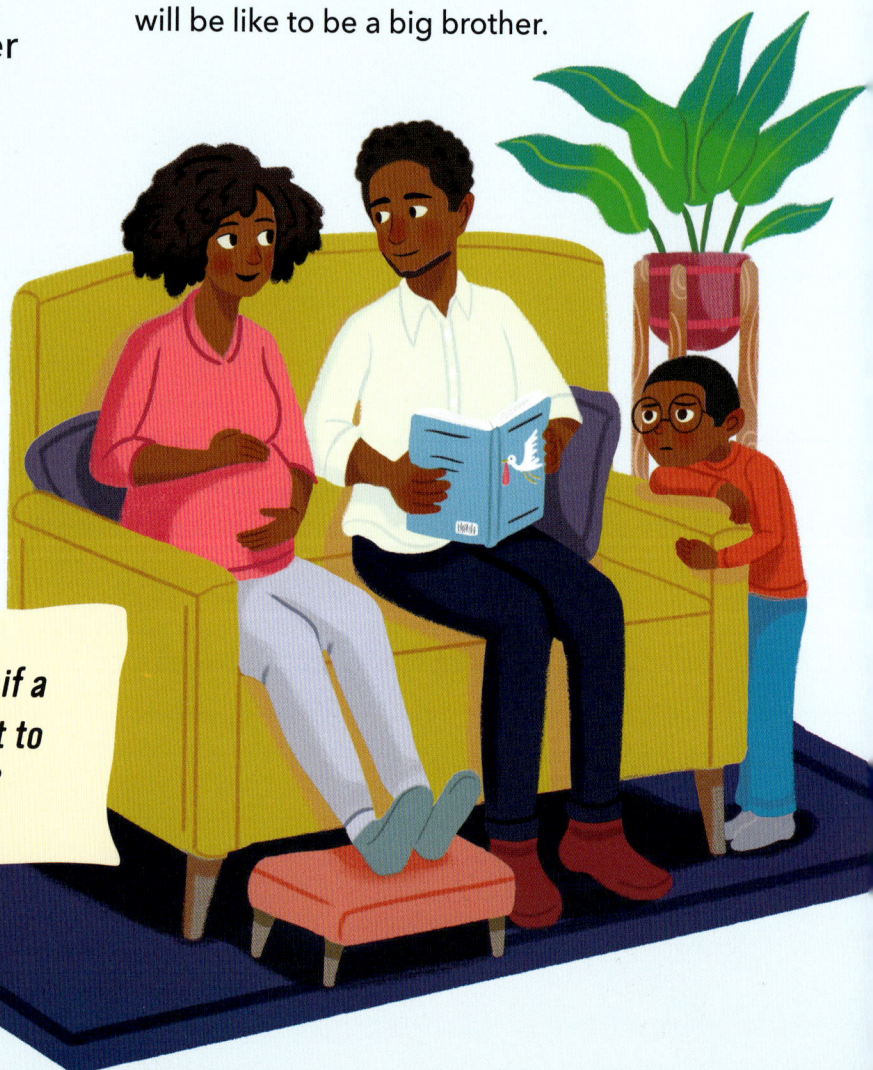

?

How would you feel if a new baby was about to join your family?

Foster Parents

Some parents love their children but cannot look after them properly for all sorts of reasons. Other parents may be hurting their children. When this happens, the children are sometimes placed with foster parents. They look after them until they can go home, or until a new family can adopt them.

Martin and Tom adopted Josh, Ben and Lewis when their mother could not look after them anymore. They give them lots of love and attention.

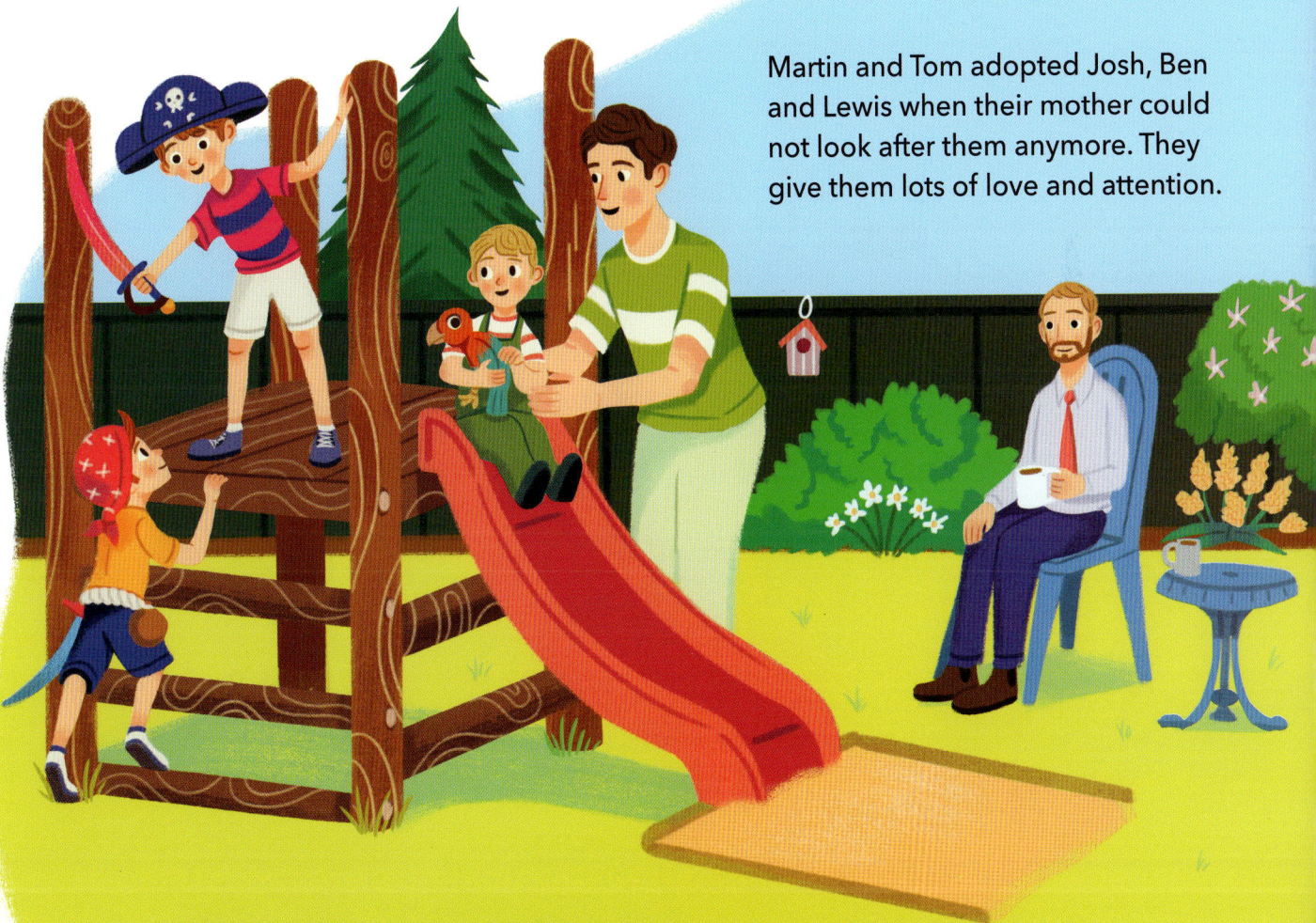

Adopting Children

Sometimes children are adopted after they have spent time in a foster family. The adoptive parents become the child or children's immediate family for ever. They will care for them in a safe and loving home.

LOOKING AFTER YOU

All children need an adult to look after them and love them, to give them a place to live, to keep them safe and healthy, and to make sure they eat, sleep and go to school. A parent or two parents are usually in charge of doing these things, but sometimes they need help.

Zach's dad helps him with his maths homework after dinner. He shows Zach how to work out the answers for himself.

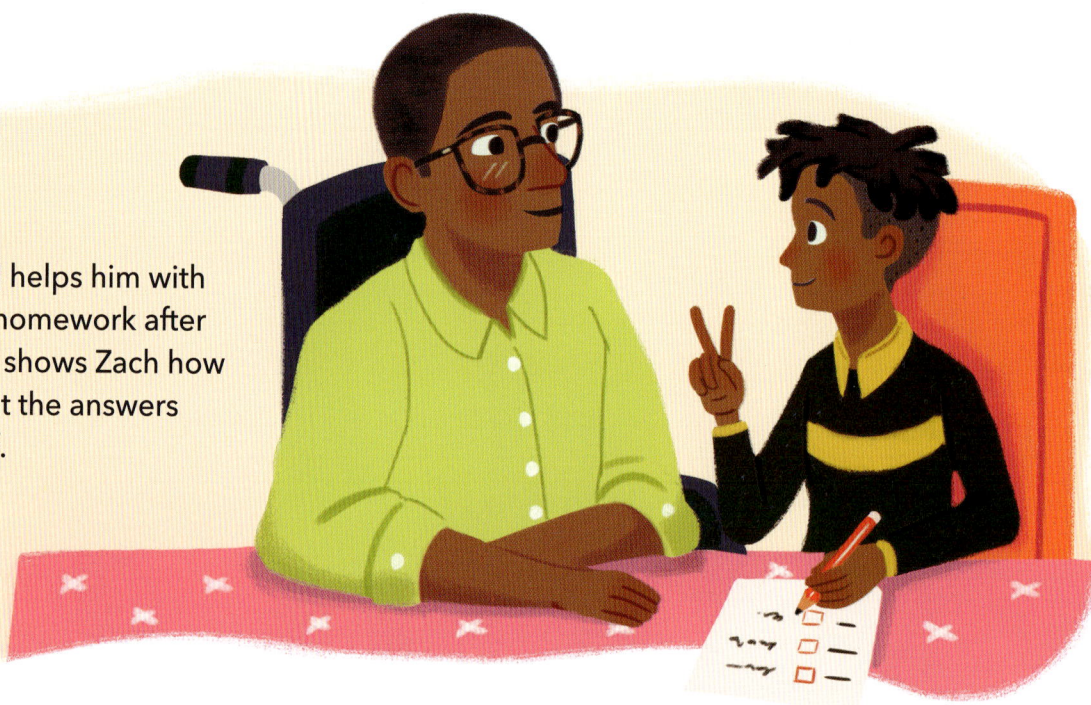

A Parent's Job

Parents act as a guide through childhood, helping their children to learn right from wrong. They try to teach and encourage their children – but also tell them off if they behave badly. Most parents agree that being a mum or dad is the best job in the world, but also the hardest. Your parents aren't perfect – they are learning how to be good parents so sometimes they can make mistakes.

Help with Childcare

Your parents may need help looking after you when they go to work. If family live nearby, grandparents or a relative might help with childcare. Some parents pay a childminder or a nanny to look after their children, while other children go to after-school clubs or breakfast clubs.

?

Who helps to look after you?

BROTHERS AND SISTERS

Many children have brothers or sisters in their family. Brothers and sisters are also called siblings. They may be older or younger than you, or the same age if you are a twin. Siblings are usually part of your immediate family.

A Special Relationship

Brothers and sisters share a special relationship. They are an important part of your life when you are children and that can continue when you are adults. Siblings can help each other, have fun together and share lots of things that are special to the family.

Harry has a big brother and a younger sister. He loves playing with them and celebrating special days.

Arguments

Your relationship with your brother or sister can be like a seesaw – sometimes up and sometimes down. You have to share your home and your toys with them, as well as your parents. Sometimes this means you fight to get attention from your parents or from one of your siblings. At other times, a brother or sister can be your best friend, someone who stands by you no matter what.

?

Do you have brothers or sisters? How do you get along?

Sometimes, Mustapha fights with his little brother, Hamza. Most of the time, they just have fun fooling around.

GRANDPARENTS

You might call them Grandma and Grandpa, Granny and Grandad, Nanna and Poppa, or something else. They are your grandparents, you mum and dad's parents or step-parents. You might even have great-grandparents – the parents of your grandparents!

Olden Days

Imagine your grandparents bringing up your parents – reminding them to tidy their room or brush their teeth – just as your parents do now.

Jacob's mum says that Granny (her mum) was strict with her when she was growing up but they also had a lot of fun. Jacob can't imagine Granny being strict!

Fun with Grandchildren

Your grandparents may live nearby or far away. Sadly, some grandparents may be ill or have died but many grandparents still enjoy time with their grandchildren. Grandparents often feel that they have already done the hard job of raising children (that's your parents) so now they can relax and spoil their grandchildren (you).

Although Lola's gran lives far away, Lola likes to chat to her using the laptop.

LOTS OF RELATIVES

How many relatives have you got? Your extended family can go on and on, with some relatives living nearby and others far away. You may not know some of your cousins, second cousins, great-aunts and great-uncles.

Who's Who of Relatives

- Aunts and uncles – your parents' brothers and sisters (including any half-siblings or step-siblings) and any partners
- Cousins – your aunts and uncles' children
- Second cousins – the children of your parents' first cousins
- Great-aunts and great-uncles – your parents' aunts and uncles
- Great-grandparents – your grandparents' parents
- Great-great aunts and great-great uncles – your great-grandparents' brothers and sisters

Every year, lots of relatives come to Natasha's family gathering.

Different Generations

You, your siblings (including half-siblings or step-siblings), cousins and step-cousins, all belong to the youngest generation. Next is your parents' generation, with your aunts and uncles, and the generation above them – your grandparents' generation with your great-uncles and great-aunts. Relatives from the past are called ancestors.

Ancestors

It can be fun to find out about your ancestors. Ask the oldest people in your family whether they have any family stories about relatives who lived in the past. They may have some old photos or documents to show you. Some families have lived in the same area for generations while others have moved around for work or other reasons.

Sometimes we think of our parents' close friends as part of the family too, and we may call them 'aunt' or 'uncle'.

AN EXTENDED FAMILY TREE

GREAT-GRANDAD and GREAT-GRANNY

GREAT-GRANDMA and GREAT-GRANDPA

Great-uncle Peter and GREAT-AUNT LINDA

GREAT-UNCLE BILL

GRANNY and GRANDAD

ELISE and Jake
(First cousin once removed)

JOHN and Becky
(First cousin once removed)

AUNTIE LUCY and Uncle Richard

MUM

ANNA
(Second cousin)

ELLA and EVIE
(Cousins)

KITTY and OLIVIA
(Second cousins)

GREAT-GRANDAD and GREAT-GRANNY

GREAT-GRANDPA and GREAT-GRANDMA

Laura's extended family tree looks huge when you write it all down. This picture shows four generations of her family and how they are related to Laura.

Great-uncle Bert and GREAT-AUNT JANE

GREAT-UNCLE MIKE

Grandpa-Jo and GRANDMA

GRANDPA

NICOLA and FRED
(First cousins once removed)

UNCLE PETER and Uncle Sam

Uncle Nick and AUNT LISA

DAD

Your mother's first cousin is your first cousin once removed, indicating the different generations.

LAURA

17

JOSH

OLLIE and BEN
(Cousins)

CHANGING FAMILIES

Families don't always stay the same. People change over time and this means that families change too. They may gain new members and lose others.

Until his baby sister was born, Jo was the youngest in his family.

Adding Family Members

When children are born or adopted, or when adults meet a new partner, new people join the family. The family has to get used to the change. Babies, for example, may be small in size but they make a big difference to the everyday life of a family, and to relationships within the family.

When Parents Separate

Sometimes parents may decide that they can no longer live together even though they both love their children. When parents separate or divorce, it affects the children too. It takes time for everyone to get used to the new life and it can be a difficult time.

Mia cried when her dad moved out. She's still getting used to the new arrangements.

Losing Family

As time passes, people get older and die. If someone in your family dies, you will probably feel sad for a long time. Others in your family will also feel sad so talk to them about your feelings. After a while, the sadness will fade but your special memories will remain.

TOGETHER AND APART

There are masses of different sorts of family. Members of the same family may live together or apart.

Dylan's parents are separated. He lives with his mum most of the time ...

... but he sees his dad at weekends and in the school holidays.

?

What kinds of things might children have to get used to if one parent moves away?

Two Homes

If parents separate, one parent usually stays with the children in the family home at the start, while the other moves out. Some children live part of the time with each parent, so they have two homes. Even though the parents live apart, they still have to work together to make sure the children are looked after properly.

Step-families

Some children are part of a step-family. If parents have separated, they may move in with someone else. The new partner becomes a step-father, or step-mother to the children that are already in the family. If the step-parents also have children, those children become step-sisters and step-brothers.

Nico's mum is married to Grace's dad, making Nico and Grace step-brother and step-sister. Last year, Nico's mum and Grace's dad had a baby together. The baby is Nico and Grace's half-sister.

Sometimes children may need to live apart from their family. They may live with a foster family or in a children's home and then return home. They may move from a foster family or children's home to live with someone in the extended family or with new parents who will adopt them.

LIVING IN A FAMILY

Even when you love your family, it can be hard to get along sometimes. It helps to think about other people, and to be kind and considerate as much as possible. Then family life will be much more pleasant!

Most of the time, Marta and Katrin like sharing and doing things together. They especially like sharing stories and giggles at bedtime.

?

What have you shared with your brother or sister recently?

Sharing

Living together involves a lot of sharing – it can be sharing a bedroom, sharing toys or a computer. It helps if you can keep things tidy and help out when asked. Another tip for family life is to ask permission before you use someone else's stuff as it will help everyone get along much better.

Sometimes Ollie and Joe fall out over stuff and their mum has to help them sort it out.

Not all the Same

Just because you are related it does not mean that everyone in your family is the same. You each have your own likes and dislikes. Although you may not agree with everyone in your family all of the time, it's important to listen to each other.

Sometimes bad things happen in families. No one has the right to hurt you or make you do something that you think is wrong. You should never be told to keep a secret that makes you feel confused or sad. If this happens, tell an adult you trust. If someone in your family is hurting you, tell an adult you trust, such as a teacher or another trusted adult, or call one of the organisations listed on page 31.

FUN FOR ALL THE FAMILY

Special occasions are times for families to gather and celebrate. People often want to share their happiness with other members of the family.

?

What special times have you celebrated with your family?

Celebrating Together

Sometimes, the entire extended family gathers together for a special occasion. Even relatives that live abroad fly in to attend special family celebrations.

Weddings

When couples marry, they promise to stay together for life. They become a family and now they are both part of each other's extended families of aunts, uncles, cousins and grandparents. The couple call each other's parents their mother-in-law and father-in-law. A sibling by marriage is a brother-in-law or sister-in-law.

Lots of relatives and friends celebrated Isobel and Lynton's wedding. They threw confetti to wish the couple good luck in their lives together as a brand-new family.

YOUR FAMILY AND YOU

Being part of a family usually means that you've got people who care about you and a place to belong. Families should love and support each other – and have fun together.

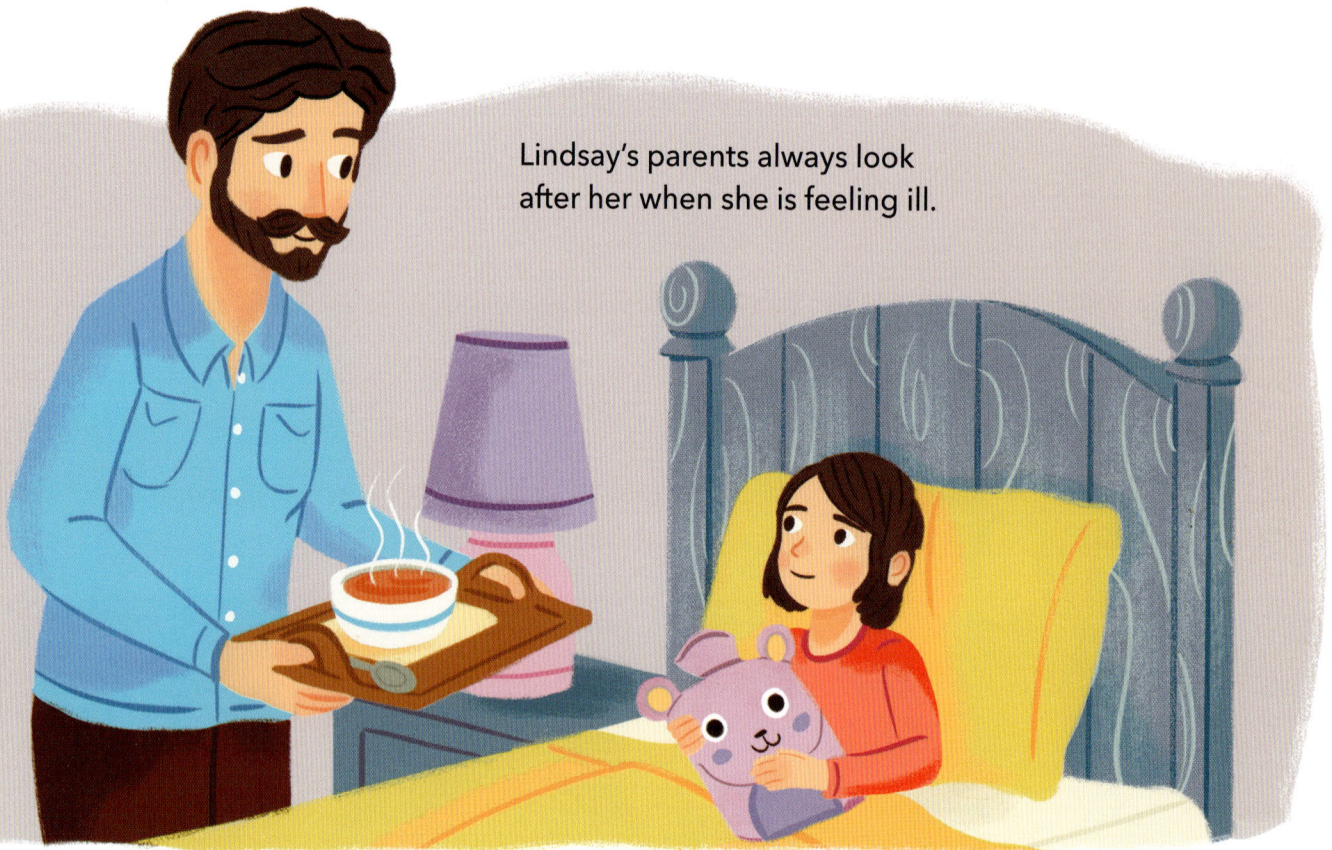

Lindsay's parents always look after her when she is feeling ill.

Helping each Other

Families should help each other and look after each other, in good times and bad. Make sure you tell them how much they mean to you. You may take it for granted that your family already knows you love them, but it's always nice to hear the words!

? Do you feel very unhappy at home with your family? Try talking to an adult you trust about your problems and feelings.

Sometimes, Manjit and Preet bake biscuits with their dad.

Time Together

Families are often very busy but simply spending time together is important. Having fun makes everyone feel good about themselves and about the other people in the family. Enjoying time together also leaves you with happy memories that you can share in years to come.

THINGS TO TALK ABOUT AND DO

Before you Begin

Talk about the people in your immediate family (siblings or step-siblings, parents or step-parents, grandparents etc). Are there any other special people in your life such as aunties, uncles, cousins, a childminder or babysitter?

Think and Talk

Changing families

Read the information about changing families on pages 18–19. Think about the changes that happen when someone joins the family. For example, when a new baby is born it might mean older children have to share a bedroom to make room for the new baby; they might have to get used to being woken up at night if the baby cries; and they have to share their parents with the new baby. What would stay the same?

What about the situation where one parent invites their new partner to live in the family home. What might change, and what would stay the same?

Write

Fun with the family

Which activities do you enjoy most with your family?
Write a list of the activities you enjoy together.

Cook dinner together

Play a game

Go for a walk in the park

Happy days

Write a diary entry recording a memory of spending time with your family. It could be about a day trip, a special time at home, or a birthday celebration – you choose.

Family tree

Make a family tree to include you and any brothers and sisters, your parents, aunts, uncles, cousins and grandparents. Look at examples of family trees in this book to help you get started.

Granny and Grandad
(Mum's mum and dad)

Grandma, Grandpa Jo and Grandpa
(Dad's mum, step-dad and dad)

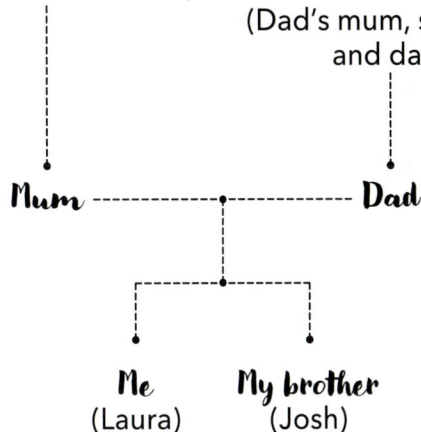

Mum -------------------- Dad

Me
(Laura)

My brother
(Josh)

Create

Family portrait

Draw a portrait of your family. Look at portraits of family groups for ideas by using the websites of art galleries. Will you include family pets if you have any?

29

GLOSSARY

adopted Become part of a family that is not the family you were born into.

ancestor Family relative from the past.

blood relative A person who is related to you by birth rather than through marriage and who shares common ancestors.

childminder Someone who is paid to look after other people's children in the childminder's home.

children's home Usually a large house where children and young people live together as a group if their parents cannot take care of them.

cousin Also called first cousin. The child of your aunt or uncle.

divorce When a couple who were married go through the process of separating completely so that they are not married any longer.

encourage To give someone help, hope and support by offering help and praise.

extended family Family members that are not as closely related to you as your parents and siblings, such as your cousins, aunts, uncles and grandparents.

family tree A way to show on paper how people in an extended family are related to each other.

foster parents People who look after children and bring them into their own family until the child goes back to his or her family, or is adopted.

generation One level of the family tree. For example, you, your brothers and sisters and first cousins are the youngest generation.

great-grandparents Your grandparents' parents (who are also your mother or father's grandparents).

half-sister or half-brother A sister or brother with whom you share one parent, but not both parents, for instance the baby whose mum is your mum, but whose dad is your new step-dad.

immediate family Family members that you live with who are usually closely related to you, such as your mum, dad, sister, brother, step-siblings or half-siblings.

partner The person someone lives with or is going out with. The couple can be married or not.

pregnant Have a baby or babies developing inside the womb.

relationships The many ways people get along with each other. For instance, you have a relationship with your mum and a different sort of relationship with your brother or sister and another sort of relationship with your grandparents or friends.

relatives/relations People who are part of your family.

second cousin The child of one of your parents' first cousins.

separate When partners in a relationship separate it means they no longer live together.

siblings Sisters or brothers. There are also half-siblings – half-brothers or half-sisters – and step-siblings – step-sisters or step-brothers.

step-brother/step-sister The son or daughter of the person one of your parents has married, or is in a relationship with.

step-dad/step-mum The person who your parent is in a relationship with (and who isn't your dad or mum).

step-family A family formed of two people and the child or children of one of them from a previous relationship. The new partner is the step-mum or step-dad of any children that were born before this new relationship started and the children are his or her step-children.

TRUSTED ADULTS

Throughout this book, the author advises you to talk to a trusted adult if you are upset, afraid or confused about something that is going on in your family life. A trusted adult is someone you are happy to be around and who listens to what you say, or someone who has helped you before. It can be many people including your teacher, a teaching assistant, a nurse, your parents, an older sibling or your grandparents. Not all adults are trusted adults.

FURTHER INFORMATION

WEBSITES IN THE UK

Childline: Childline helps anyone under the age of 19 in the UK with any issue they are going through. Call them free on 0800 1111 or go to their website at: **www.childline.org.uk**

Gingerbread: Gingerbread is a charity supporting single parent families to live secure, happy and fulfilling lives. Their website is: **www.gingerbread.org.uk**

Place2be: Place2Be is a children's mental health charity that provides counselling, support and training in UK schools. Their website is: **www.place2be.org.uk**

Save the Children: The charity, Save the Children, has developed a programme called 'Families Connect' to support parents and children to learn together. For more information, look on their website at: **www.savethechildren.org.uk/what-we-do/uk-work/in-schools/families-connect**

WEBSITES IN AUSTRALIA

Kidshelp: Kidshelp offers free and confidential phone and online counselling to young people aged 5 to 25 and also supports parents and families. Call them free on 1800 55 1800 or go to their website at: **www.kidshelp.com.au**

Save the Children: The charity, Save the Children, has been supporting Australian children and children around the world for over a hundred years. Their website is: **www.savethechildren.org.au**

NCSMC: The National Council for Single Mothers and their Children offers support to single mothers. Their website is: **www.ncsmc.org.au**

Download a resource kit for rainbow families at: **http://jacquitomlins.com/outspoken-families-a-resource-kit-for-rainbow-families**

INDEX